How To Be An Up Person in a Down World

How to Stop Worrying & Start Living

HB HONOR BOOKS

Honor Books, Inc. • P.O. Box 55388 • Tulsa, OK 74155

7th Printing

How To Be an Up Person in a Down World
ISBN 1-56292-052-9

P. O. Box 55388
Tulsa, OK 74155

INTRODUCTION

How To Be an Up Person in a Down World is an inspirational collection of quotes that will challenge you to be positive in a negative world. Taking the best motivational quotes and putting them into an easy-to-read format, this book gives you a quick source of wisdom to fire you up and lead you down the path to real success.

This delightful book contains an enthusiasm for God's best that is hard to resist. It was designed to help you achieve all that God wants for you. Fun to read, yet thought inspiring, this book is filled with quotes and sayings that will encourage you to reach for the best and fulfill your God-given potential.

This is not just a book of cute sayings about daily living, rather it touches on the areas that daily shape your life. From integrity in business to overcoming failure, this little book offers insight and motivation to help you succeed in life. *How To Be an Up Person in a Down World* can be a place of fresh beginnings and continual inspiration. We at Honor Books hope that you will learn to enjoy, remember and turn to the sayings in this book as much as we have.

Remember, now is the time — *stop worrying and start living!*

Yesterday is a cancelled check;
tomorrow is a promissory note;
today is the only cash you have,
so spend it wisely.

-Kay Lyons

Problems are only opportunities
in work clothes.

-Henry Kaiser

Neither the wise man nor
a brave man lies down on the
tracks of history to wait
for the train of the future
to run over him.

-Dwight D. Eisenhower

Give me a stock clerk with a goal, and I will give you a man who will make history. Give me a man without a goal, and I will give you a stock clerk.

-J. C. Penney

You cannot escape the responsibility of tomorrow by evading it today.

-Abraham Lincoln

It is kind of fun to do the impossible.

-Walt Disney

The good news is that the bad news can be turned into good news when you change your attitude!

-Robert Schuller

People can succeed at almost anything for which they have unlimited enthusiasm.

-Charles Schwab

Try not to become a man of success but rather try to become a man of value.

-Albert Einstein

Rule #1: Don't sweat the small stuff.
Rule #2: It's all small stuff.

-Dr. Michael Mantell

Remember, no one can make you feel inferior without your consent.

-Eleanor Roosevelt

The key to everything is patience. You get the chicken by hatching the egg. . . not by smashing it.

-Arnold Glasow

Life is an echo. What you send out - - you get back. What you give -- you get.

Impossibilities vanish when a man and his God confront a mountain.

-Robert Schuller

You can make more friends in two months by becoming interested in other people than you can in two years of trying to get other people interested in you.

-Dale Carnegie

Character may be manifested in the great moments, but it is made in the small ones.

-Phillips Brooks

Learn to laugh at your troubles and you'll never run out of things to laugh at.

-Lyn Karol

Between saying and doing many a pair of shoes is worn out.

-Italian Proverb

A great deal of good can be done in the world if one is not too careful who gets the credit.

-A Jesuit Motto

Whether you think you can or you think you can't, you are right.

-Henry Ford

If you keep saying that things are going to be bad, you have a chance of being a prophet.

-Isaac Singer

It is never too late to be what you might have been.

-George Elliot

The greatest use of life is to spend it for something that will outlast it.

-William James

I don't know the secret to success but the key to failure is to try to please everyone.

-Bill Cosby

My obligation is to do the right thing. The rest is in God's hands.

-Martin Luther King

The safe way to double your money is to fold it over once and put it in your pocket.

-Frank Hubbard

For all your days prepare, and meet them ever alike: when you are the anvil, bear -- when you are the hammer, strike.

-Edwin Markham

Hating people is like burning down your own house to get rid of a rat.

-Harry Emerson Fosdick

Some cause happiness wherever they go; others whenever they go.

I don't know anything about luck. I've never banked on it, and I'm afraid of people who do. Luck to me is something else; hard work and realizing what is opportunity and what isn't.

Lucille Ball

The indispensable first step to getting the things you want out of life is this; decide what you want.

-Ben Stein

What lies behind us and what lies before us are tiny matters compared to what lies within us.

-Ralph Waldo Emerson

Promises may get friends but ´tis performance that keeps them.

-Benjamin Franklin

Not everything that is faced can be changed, but nothing can be changed until it is faced.

-James Baldwin

I will not permit any man to narrow and degrade my soul by making me hate him.

-Booker T. Washington

There is little difference in people, but that little difference makes a big difference. The little difference is attitude. The big difference is whether it is positive or negative.

-W. Clement Stone

A man is not old until regrets take the place of dreams.

-John Barrymore

The Constitution of America only guarantees pursuit of happiness; you have to catch up with it yourself.

-Gill Robb Wilson

I so desire to conduct the affairs of this administration that if at the end, when I come to lay down the reins of power, I have lost every other friend on earth, I shall at least have one friend left, and that friend shall be down inside of me.

-Abraham Lincoln

Character is the ability to carry out a good resolution long after the excitement of the moment has passed.

-Cavett Robert

Laughter is a tranquilizer with no side effects.

-Arnold Glasow

. . . Small deeds done are better than great deeds planned.

-Peter Marshall

It's nothing against you to fall down flat, but to lie there -- that's disgrace.

-Edmund Vance Cooke

Outside show is a poor substitute for inner worth.

-Aesop

When one door of happiness closes, another opens; but often we look so long at the closed door that we do not see the one that has been opened for us.

-Helen Keller

Failure doesn't mean you are a failure. . .
. it just means you haven't succeeded yet.

-Robert Schuller

A pessimist is one who makes difficulties of his opportunities; an optimist is one who makes opportunities of his difficulties.

-Reginald B. Mansell

People who fight fire with fire usually end up with ashes.

-Abigail Van Buren

Joy is the feeling of grinning inside.

-Dr. Melba Colgrove

A merry heart doeth good like a medicine.

-Proverbs 27:22 (KJV)

It is not the going out of port,
but the coming in that
determines the success
of a voyage.

-Henry Ward Beecher

Sometimes a winner is just a dreamer who never gave up.

Even if you're on the right track, you'll get run over if you just sit there.

-Will Rogers

Fix your thoughts on what is true and good and right. Think about things that are pure and lovely, and dwell on the fine, good things in others. Think about all you can praise God for and be glad about it.

-Philippians 4:8 (TLB)

Unless you enter the tiger's den you cannot take the cubs.

-Japanese Proverb

You see things and you say "Why?" I dream things that never were and say "Why not?"

-George Bernard Shaw

Every tomorrow has two handles. You can take hold of the handle of anxiety or the handle of enthusiasm. Upon your choice so will be the day.

"One of these days" is *none* of these days.

-English Proverb

He that riseth late must trot all day.

-Benjamin Franklin

Perhaps the most valuable result of all education is the ability to make yourself do the thing you have to do, when it ought to be done whether you like it or not.

-Thomas Huxley

Business is like a wheelbarrow. Nothing ever happens until you start pushing.

Our dignity is not in what we *do* but in who we *are.*

A critic is a man who knows the way but can't drive the car.

-Kenneth Tynan

When you handle yourself, use your head; when you handle others, use your heart.

-Donna Reed

In life, as in football, you won't go far unless you know where the goalposts are.

-Arnold Glasow

Do not follow where the path may lead -- go instead where there is no path and leave a trail.

The foolish man seeks happiness in the distance; the wise grows it under his feet.

-James Openheim

If God is for us, who can be against us?

-Romans 8:31b (NIV)

Whatever the majority of people is doing, under any given circumstance, if you do the exact opposite, you will probably never make another mistake as long as you live.

-Earl Nightingale

Dost thou love life? Then do not squander time, for that is the stuff life is made of.

-Benjamin Franklin

Genius is one percent inspiration and ninety-nine percent perspiration.

-Thomas Alva Edison

That old law about "an eye for an eye" leaves everybody blind.

-Martin Luther King

Some people are always grumbling because roses have thorns; I am thankful that thorns have roses.

-Alphonse Karr

Millions saw the apple fall, but Newton was the one who asked why.

-Bernard Baruch

I have noticed that nothing
I have *never* said ever did
me any harm.

-Calvin Coolidge

How much pain have cost us the evils which have never happened!

-Thomas Jefferson

If you are all wrapped up in yourself, you are overdressed.

-Kate Halverson

No race can prosper till it learns there is as much dignity in tilling a field as in writing a poem.

-Booker T. Washington

It is a mistake to look too far ahead. Only one link of the chain of destiny can be handled at a time.

-Winston Churchill

There is no substitute for hard work.

-Thomas Edison

Until you make peace with who you are, you'll never be content with what you have.

-Doris Mortman

When I look into the future, it's so bright it burns my eyes.

-Oprah Winfrey

Shallow men believe in luck. . . Strong men believe in cause and effect.

-Emerson

Happiness is produced not so much by great pieces of good fortune that seldom happen as by little advantages that occur every day.

-Benjamin Franklin

Today well lived makes every yesterday a dream of happiness, and every tomorrow a vision of hope.

There is no pit so deep that Jesus is not deeper still.

-Corrie Ten Boom

The spirit, the will to win, and the will to excel are the things that endure. These qualities are so much more important than the events that occur.

-Vince Lombardi

To avoid criticism, do nothing, say nothing, be nothing.

-Elbert Hubbard

Nobody has ever expected me to be President.

-Abraham Lincoln

Hope is the feeling you have that the feeling you have isn't permanent.

-Jean Kerr

He who receives a good turn should never forget it; he who does one should never remember it.

-Charron

People may doubt what you say, but they will believe what you do.

Destiny is not a matter of chance, it is a matter of choice. It is not a thing to be waited for; it is a thing to be achieved.

-William Jennings Bryan

The journey of a thousand miles begins with a single step.

It took me a long time not to judge myself through someone else's eyes.

-Sally Field

May the Lord bless and protect you, may the Lord's face radiate with joy because of you. May He be gracious to you, show you His favor and give you His peace.

-Numbers 6:24-26 (NIV)

Happiness is a direction, not a place.

-Sydney J. Harris

The miracle is this. . . the more we share, the more we have.

-Leonard Nimoy

Men are born with two eyes but with one tongue, in order that they should see twice as much as they say.

-Charles Caleb Colton

No one is useless in this world who lightens the burden of it to anyone else.

-Charles Dickens

A day hemmed in prayer is less likely to unravel.

Laziness travels so slowly, that poverty soon overtakes him.

-Benjamin Franklin

Experience is the name everyone gives to their mistakes.

-Oscar Wilde

You can never plan the future by the past.

-Edmund Burke

All our dreams can come true --
if we have the courage
to pursue them.

-Walt Disney

None will improve your lot, if you yourselves do not.

-Bertolt Brecht

The greatest achievements are those that benefit others.

-Denis Waitley

The ultimate measure of a man is not where he stands in moments of comfort and convenience, but where he stands at times of challenge and controversy.

-Martin Luther King

Give others a piece of your heart,
not a piece of your mind.

As long as you're green, you're growing;
as soon as you're ripe you start to rot.

-Ray Kroc

Plenty of people miss their share of happiness, not because they never found it, but because they didn't stop to enjoy it.

-W. Feather

It's better to keep one's mouth shut and be thought a fool than to open it and resolve all doubt.

-Abraham Lincoln

We cannot be sure that we have something worth living for unless we are ready to die for it.

-Eric Hoffer

We have to learn to be our own best friends because we fall too easily into the trap of being our own worst enemies.

-Roderick Thorpe

The most wasted of all our days are those in which we have not laughed.

-Sebastien Chamfort

If you want to lift yourself up, lift up someone else.

-Booker T. Washington

Nothing is "opened by mistake" more than the mouth.

Great minds have purpose;
others have wishes.

-Washington Irving

In the race to be better or best, don't forget to enjoy the journey!

Unhappiness is in not knowing what we want and killing ourselves to get it.

-Don Herold

In the depth of winter I finally learned that within me there lay an invincible summer.

-Albert Camus

You may give out, but never give up.

-Mary Crowley

Happiness is inward, and not outward; and so, it does not depend on what we have, but on what we are.

-Henry Van Dyke

Whatever you do today,
do it better tomorrow.

-Robert Schuller

The greatest discovery of my generation is that human beings can alter their lives by altering their attitudes of mind.

-William James

Good habits are not made on birthdays, nor Christian character at the New Year. The workshop of character is everyday life. The uneventful and commonplace hour is where the battle is lost or won.

Always do right -- this will gratify some and astonish the rest.

-Mark Twain

Men of few words are the best men.

-Shakespeare

When written in Chinese, the word "crisis" is composed of two characters -- one represents danger and the other represents opportunity.

Far and away the best prize that life offers is the chance to work hard at work worth doing.

-Theodore Roosevelt

People are always neglecting something they can do in trying to do something they can't.

-Edgar Watson Howe

I am more and more convinced that our happiness or unhappiness depends far more on the way we meet the events of life than on the nature of those events themselves.

-Wilhelm Von Humbolt

A man is known by the company his mind keeps.

-Thomas Bailey Aldrich

Joy is the holy fire that keeps our purpose warm and our intelligence aglow.

-Helen Keller

You can have anything you want. . . if you want it badly enough. You can be anything you want to be, having anything you desire, accomplish anything you set out to accomplish. . . if you will hold to that desire with singleness of purpose.

-Robert Collier

Every calling is great when greatly pursued.

-Oliver Wendell Holmes

Live truth instead of professing it.

-Elbert Hubbard

The heart of a fool is in his mouth but the mouth of a wise man is in his heart.

-Benjamin Franklin

There are periods when to dare, is the highest wisdom.

-William Ellery Channing

By all means, don't say, "If I can;" say, "I will."

-Abraham Lincoln

The darkest hour is only 60 minutes.

Big people monopolize the listening.
Small people monopolize the talking.

-David Schwartz

Truth is generally the best
vindication against slander.

-Abraham Lincoln

May you live all the days of your life.

-Jonathan Swift

The man who makes no mistakes does not usually make anything.

-William Conner Magee

There is no failure except in no longer trying.

-Elbert Hubbard

Nothing will ever be attempted if all possible objections must first be overcome.

-Samuel Johnson

Failure is the opportunity to begin again more intelligently.

-Henry Ford

Life lived for tomorrow will always be just a day away from being realized.

-Leo Buscaglia

Don't let your learning lead to knowledge, let your learning lead to action.

-Jim Rohn

Worry never robs tomorrow of its sorrow, it only saps today of its joy.

-Leo Buscaglia

The art of being wise is the art of knowing what to overlook.

-William James

Don't worry about anything; instead, pray about everything; tell God your needs and don't forget to thank Him for His answers. If you do this you will experience God's peace, which is far more wonderful than the human mind can understand.

-Philippians 4:6-7 (TLB)

When you look for the good in others you discover the best in yourself.

-Martin Walsh

Hold fast to dreams, for if dreams die, life is a broken winged bird that cannot fly.

-Langston Hughes

We tend to forget that happiness doesn't come as a result of getting something we don't have, but rather of recognizing and appreciating what we do have.

-Frederick Keonig

Of all the things you wear, your expression is the most important.

-Janet Lane

If things go wrong, don't go with them.

-Roger Babson

In order to succeed, you must know what you are doing, like what you are doing and believe in what you are doing.

-Will Rogers

Success consists of a series of little daily efforts.

-Mamie McCullough

"I can't do it" never yet accomplished anything; "I will try" has performed wonders.

-George P. Burnham

You will find as you look back upon your life that the moments that stand out, the moments when you have really lived, are the moments when you have done things in a spirit of love.

-Henry Drummond

Age may wrinkle the face, but lack of enthusiasm wrinkles the soul.

Be a leader: remember the lead sled dog is the only one with a decent view.

All I have seen teaches me to trust the Creator for all I have not seen.

-Emerson

Success seems to be largely a matter of hanging on after others have let go.

-William Feather

Success seems to be connected with action. Successful people keep moving. They make mistakes, but they don't quit.

-Conrad Hilton

Life is no brief candle to me. It is a sort of splendid torch which I have got hold of for a moment, and I want to make it burn as brightly as possible before handing it on to future generations.

-George Bernard Shaw

No wind favors him who has no destined port.

-Michel De Montaigne

Life is not so short but that there is always time for courtesy.

-Ralph Waldo Emerson

People are always blaming their circumstances for what they are. I don't believe in circumstances. The people who get on in this world are the people who get up and look for the circumstances they want, and, if they can't find them, make them.

-George Bernard Shaw

You have removed most of the roadblocks to success when you have learned the difference between movement and direction.

-Joe L. Griffith

To succeed, jump as quickly at opportunities as you do at conclusions.

-Benjamin Franklin

Cheerfulness oils the machinery of life.

Do the thing you fear and the death of fear is certain.

Courage is fear that has said its prayers.

The way each day will look to you all starts with *who* you're looking to.

If Columbus would have turned back, no one would have blamed him. Of course, no one would have remembered him either.

A goal is nothing more tha a dream with a time limit.

-Joe L. Griffith

Experience is what you get when you don't get what you want.

-Dan Stanford

Personality has the power to open many doors, but character keeps them open.

No man becomes rich unless he enriches others.

-Andrew Carnegie

A strong passion for any object will ensure success, for the desire of the end will point out the means.

-William Hazlitt

He who considers his work beneath him will be above doing it well.

-Alexander Chase

Men for the sake of getting a living forget to live.

-Margaret Fuller

None is so deaf as he that will not hear.

-Thomas Fuller, M.D.

Wisdom is *always* an overmatch for strength.

-Phaedrus

The conduct of our lives is the true mirror of our doctrine.

-Montaigne

The bigger a man's head, the worse his headache.

-Persian Proverb

It is neither wealth nor splendor but tranquility and occupation which give happiness.

-Thomas Jefferson

Man is not made for defeat.

-Earnest Hemingway

The future has several names. For the weak it is the impossible. For the fainthearted it is the unknown. For the thoughtful and valiant it is the ideal.

-Victor Hugo

Mix a conviction with a man and something happens.

-Adam Clayton Powell

Vision is the art of seeing things invisible.

-Jonathan Swift

One of the greatest discoveries a man makes, one of his great surprises, is to find he can do what he was afraid he couldn't do.

-Henry Ford

Whatsoever thy hand findeth to do, do it with thy might.

-Ecclesiastes 9:10a (KJV)

Be great in little things.

-St. Francis Xavier

Waste your money and you're only out of money, but waste your time and you've lost a part of your life.

-Michael Leboeuf

Well done is better than well said.

-Benjamin Franklin

The price of success is much lower than the price of failure.

-Thomas Watson

There is a loftier ambition than merely to stand high in the world. It is to stoop down and lift mankind a little higher.

-Henry Van Dyke

In great attempts it is glorious even to fail.

-Vince Lombardi

Don't just make a living, design a life.

-Jim Rohn

It has been my observation that most people get ahead during the time that others waste.

-Henry Ford

Always bear in mind that your own resolution to succeed is more important than any other one thing.

-Abraham Lincoln

The poorest man is not he who is without a cent, but he who is without a dream.

-Pennsylvania School Journal

If you tell the truth, you don't have to remember anything.

-Mark Twain

The size of your success is determined by the size of your belief.

-David J. Schwartz

Minds are like parachutes: they only function when open.

-Thomas R. Dewar

It's not whether you get knocked down; it's whether you get up again.

-Vince Lombardi

I skate to where the puck is going to be, not to where it has been.

-Wayne Gretzky

Never, never, never . . . give up.

-Winston Churchill

When I hear somebody sigh, "Life is hard," I am always tempted to ask, "Compared to what?"

-Sydney J. Harris

Troubles are a lot like people -- they grow bigger if you nurse them.

Dreams don't work unless you do.

-Peter Daniels

A contented person is the one who enjoys the scenery along the detours.

Speak kind words and you will hear kind echoes.

Never miss an opportunity to make others happy; even if you have to leave them alone in order to do it.

One can never consent to creep when one feels an impulse to soar.

-Helen Keller

I had the blues because I had no shoes until upon the street, I met a man who had no feet.

-Denis Waitely

The impossible: What nobody can do until somebody does.

Luck is a matter of preparation meeting opportunity.

The trouble with life in the fast lane is that you get to the other end in an awful hurry.

-John Jensen

Standing in the middle of the road is very dangerous; you get knocked down by the traffic from both sides.

-Margaret Thatcher

It's nice to be important but it's more important to be nice.

-Trini Lopez

Life is a grindstone. Whether it grinds you down or polishes you up depends on what you are made of.

He that would have the fruit must climb the tree.

-Thomas Fuller, M.D.

The best preparation for good work tomorrow is to do good work today.

-Elbert Hubbard

The best way out of a difficulty is through it.

The worst evil of all is to leave the ranks of the living before one dies.

-Seneca

. . . The joy of the Lord is your strength.

-Nehemiah 8:10 (NIV)

Dear Reader:

If you would like to share with us a couple of your favorite quotes on the subject of *motivation* we'd love to hear from you. Our address is:

Honor Books
P. O. Box 55388, Dept. J.
Tulsa, Oklahoma 74155

Additional copies of this book and other
portable book titles
are available at your local bookstore.

God's Little Instruction Book series by Honor Books
Don't Wait for Your Ship to Come In by Honor Books
The Making of a Champion by Mike Murdock
Mama's Rules for Livin' by Mamie McCullough
Winning 101 by Van Crouch
Leadership 101 by John Maxwell
Momentum Builders by John Mason

P. O. Box 55388
Tulsa, OK 74155